Edith Jacobson Begins to Fly

and other poems

by Patricia Zontelli

1990 Minnesota Voices Project Winner

New Rivers Press 1992

Copyright © 1992 by Patricia Zontelli
Library of Congress Catalog Card Number 91-61258
ISBN 0-89823-133-7
All Rights Reserved
Edited by C. W. Truesdale
Editorial Assistance by Paul J. Hintz
Cover drawing by Patricia Zontelli
Book Design and Typesetting by Peregrine Publications

Some of the poems in *Edith Jacobson Begins to Fly and Other Poems* originally appeared, in somewhat different versions, in the following publications: *The Cumberland Poetry Review*, *The Gettysburg Review*, *Great River Review*, *The Hiram Poetry Review*, *Kansas Quarterly*, *Passages North*, *Plainswoman*, *Wisconsin Review*, and *Writing Women*. Our thanks to the editors of these publications for allowing us to reprint the works here.

The publication of *Edith Jacobson Begins to Fly and Other Poems* has been made possible by grants from the Jerome Foundation and the Metropolitan Regional Arts Council (from an appropriation by the Minnesota Legislature). Additional support has been provided by the Arts Development Fund of the United Arts Council, the First Bank System Foundation, Liberty State Bank, the Star Tribune/Cowles Media Company, the Tennant Company Foundation, and the National Endowment for the Arts (with funds appropriated by the Congress of the United States). New Rivers Press also wishes to acknowledge the Minnesota Non-Profits Assistance Fund for its invaluable support.

New Rivers Press books are distributed by

The Talman Company
150 Fifth Avenue
New York, NY 10011

Bookslinger
2402 University Avenue West
Saint Paul, MN 55114

Edith Jacobson Begis to Fly and Other Poems has been manufactured in the United States of America for New Rivers Press, 420 N. 5th Street/Suite 910, Minneapolis, MN 55401 in a first edition of 1,200 copies.

*In memory of my parents,
Ruth and Ted Zontelli*

For Charles, Caitlin and Phaedra

Contents

1   Falling

Section I:
Edith Jacobson Begins to Fly

5   Edith Knows
6   Edith Gets a Divorce
7   Edith Jacobson Begins to Fly
9   Edith Remembers to Breathe
10   Edith Gets Rid of the Furniture
11   Clear Nights
12   Could This Be True?
13   Out
14   Examining Childhood
15   Edith at Fourteen
16   Edith Jogging Backwards
17   Flying over the Houses
19   Edith in Her Element
20   The Necessity of Light
21   Wake Me. I'm Running Out of Dreams.

Section II:
Black Car

25   Vision
26   Strangers—Late Summer Day
27   Looking in Windows
28   Snow
29   Holding
30   Violence
31   Things
32   Television
33   In an Instant
35   The Distant Flickering
37   Black Car

Section III:
Reconciliation Viewed from Great Distance

- 41 Greek Vases
- 43 Going to Work
- 44 After the Argument
- 45 Shifting
- 46 Insulation
- 47 Waiting for White
- 48 Whitewash
- 49 Ceremony
- 50 Reconciliation Viewed from Great Distance
- 51 End of a Day, End of a Summer
- 52 Builders
- 53 Night Fabrics
- 54 Grandmother Poaching Pears with Cloves
- 56 Polio: 1953
- 57 The Parents Are Leaving
- 58 Veterans Hospital—1989
- 59 Visiting the Graves—February

Section IV:
Words

- 63 It Hid Motionless Like
- 64 You Cannot Believe
- 65 Twiddle with Its
- 66 One Green One Red Lens: Serial in Five Parts
- 68 Words

Falling

Dilapidated barns falling to the earth
cow's knees buckling to kneel

to this ground:
northern Minnesota, winter, 1951.

A woman out of my past enters a steamy
rose-papered parlor carrying six frozen white

shirts. Before removing scarf or coat,
the shirts are stood round room's edge

to thaw. In minutes, they fall in on themselves
with the slow doomed reflex of shot prisoners.

Seconds before they topple, long red arms
reach to catch them, carry them to the table

for ironing: six white shirts for the man with
bad luck in his face — traveling, selling

tractor parts six days a week while she keeps their
small farm from slipping: mending fence, roof, shirt,

heart with equal fever, voice sharp
as hoe's edge.   Strong sun

and light snowfall spin outside her window.
            With that look, perpetually,

of seeing me for the first time, she works
me into my snowsuit, into my skates and out

the door onto the pond: *Skate!* she orders
as I take steps over the ice, walking

on the quick blades beneath until I slip
into that habit of gliding — longer and longer —

forward into a life where the best I can do
is stubbornly resist this dream:

myself, stumbling over and over.

Section I:

Edith Jacobson Begins to Fly

Edith Knows

Edith, under her clothesline,
views the neighborhood houses:
sturdy, permanent, stable

—even their white paint is
illusory. The wind, coming
half alive, starts tossing

the arms of her apple tree, starts
lightly lifting Edith's hair
to stand it on end—

giving her wings. The sun sudden
in the sky. For one moment
all the windows open wide,

the houses airing,
the sky transparent and glowing,
the damp in the basement

clearing its throat and considering
the stairs, considering the zig-
zag up and out of there.

Edith Gets a Divorce

The sumac bleeds
under a low raw sky

growing closer and closer
to tears as the earth spins.

She needs to warm her hands.
Or run. No small decisions:

how to begin again
or become more. What to keep

and what to lose:
the lace tablecloths, his

old clothes,
the memories snoring

next to her for 20 years,
a framed snapshot

of them by a picket fence
years before the breaking

and breaking. Edith
takes a big breath, leans

into the wind,
thinks of her lightweight

body, her thin sagging
breasts.

Her strong bones.

Edith Jacobson Begins to Fly

Six nights it has rained, steadily
as a horse racing, continuing

as if it meant a great deal
                    to continue

as if something could be won
by all this spillage.

Tonight, lightning whips the dark
over the tossing trees.

I dream myself into a clearing,
all that surrounds me rinsed, dry.

At my feet, a small motionless pool
brimming like an eye.

Distant thunder
starts to roll from deep in my throat

as I break for the hills,
begin the curious ascent.

                  *

It's like nothing I know—first,
the small stinging sparks, then

lift-off: my heart spins
beneath my ribs, I cannot breathe. Is

this what "accident" means?
I hang from nothing over everything,

rising up over my own backyard,
my own apple tree, see

how a shape curves into
what's next to it — houses

into the laps of valleys,
scrolls of woodsmoke lingering over

chimneybowls, and the slinky, licorice roads
tying it all together, everything dependent

on what is next to it — earth below,
sky above and — in between —

the circling dream.

Edith Remembers to Breathe

And then this: my arms
lift, my chest fills

and I chop away from my
clipped, hardened anger

to enter
the hole in the clouds

that will be my beginning,
that — as I near it —

looks more and more valuable,
full of skylight and air

in such wasteful abundance
there is more than enough.

Miles below, in every green
direction, the fields are open,

the tall grass dances lush
and unmanageable, all the houses

with their too-small rooms
tilting farther and farther

into the distance.

Edith Gets Rid of the Furniture

Now my days are like new rooms —
all the locks clicked open, walls

fallen away, the house dissolves
behind me so softly, so calmly

chairs float and tables, upside
down, twirl. Everything that was

near breaking point now hums:
released at last, the dark vase

has freed its flowers, the rippling
carpet unlooped its plush motifs. See

how weightless we are I sing
as lamps, beds, teacups spin into

the great garden of space. See how
gracefully we are

putting on our wings to move
into the important weather

the rough thrill of fear
rushing through our bones.

Clear Nights

On clear nights when I plunge
and bank into the dead calm air

I begin to believe that at this speed
I'll soon enter my soul:

flying in the black
above shimmering cities

I think how I belong here
and begin to sing —

down below, my old self
sits breathing quietly amidst trees

and houses; the fields stretching on
to a sea that spills over itself

making new boundaries, erasing
outlines, traces of history.

Could This Be True?

                              —that each of us
moves toward a focus so bright

and inescapable, rising
higher and higher until we see

in ways we've only dreamt. Think
of first silver notes tickling

far, far back in damp caves
of throats. Imagine

lifting away from our lives, miles of blue
so far below we make no shadow

so far up we cannot see the way
the planet is turning on itself

ruined forests, the growing piles
of ticking war toys—all are mirages

or mistakes our eyes make
and we are as blameless as this thin, thin air.

Out

No hiding now – I have entered
working space –

once this space opened
those seeds

held so tightly within me
have like wings expanded

and the trees, wisdom
spiraling inside their bark

point me in one direction: *up*
– what has been released

cannot be put back.

Examining Childhood

I circle above it for hours

    My mother

the great sad tree outside my bedroom

    leans over

to look at the girl reading her comic

    and the girl dreams:

    bullet breasts

muscular wrists   the belligerent stare

    that stuns all evil.

    The girl

gets up to leave her home   to soar

above houses and ploughed fields entering

    danger and starlight

her long moonstrides taking her over

    the dark shape

that unbends, stands tall outside her window

    nodding *yes, yes*

Edith at Fourteen

Down there a young girl gazes up at the sky, the black sky blank about to turn on, a small sigh escaping from the deepest part of her, her gaze narrowing to a stare

so sharp a star ignites—then another and another and on and on until the sky is dizzy. She thinks of the distance of stars, imagines swimming through dark to touch

them, what they would tell—her future, the hour where someone falls in love and she falls in love. The young girl down there thinks how good it is to look at something that won't look back, each star separate—acute and lonely and significant—*oh if she could hold one in her palm.*

A car door slams. A cricket clicks by her foot. The hour is cold and she is tired. How enormous the sky when everyone has gone to bed.

Edith Jogging Backwards

You remember this, don't you? —
us running the same ground over and over,
the myths of the straight line
and doing what you're told

how the face stays like that
if not careful. Sometimes, I miss you
but not the stones, the rolling boulders.

Now, I spend my sleeping hours running,
my muscles like pumps
pulling the chalk road of memory:
the blue house with no door

a red bird in its chimney stinging
again and again against its black tomb
as I slip past the house, past the red bird

into a night carelessly unfolding a story
where everything ends up all right:
a road stretching before me like a grin,
happiness, whatever it is I am

running toward, about to be found.

Flying over the Houses

                    Over houses
over empty-handed oak trees

watching autumn fail to
cold November

watching perfectly good things
die:

light   color   heat.
Down there, people withdraw

banking on late-summer
warmth and color

taken in beside
September apple trees

as they snapped late beans or
stretched high for the red fruit

or — before that —
on a steamy August lake

as they fished and watched
a black loon prow

through emerald algae.
                    February

when it is cold (so still you
think you hear thought)

one of them paints a milk-can
bright blue with sparks of yellow

like fireflies; someone else
whittles a deer

and when he is finished, paints
its body black —

antlers brilliant with green.

Edith in Her Element

Not many birds fly this high —
the ones that do

are loners. I can see far, far below me
the level V of geese, ducks — perhaps

whistling swans. At such distance
they are remote:

they could be fish.
Or bobby pins.

                    My favorite bird
is the white seagull I call Harry —

he reminds me of a friend, Harry,
who sails, never with

anyone, never talks about it, spends all
his bricklayer money on it:

he could not live if he could not sail.
Here comes another favorite, Eleanor

Roosevelt, bald-headed eagle. She's not
a performer but she keeps on doing it,

doing it: dipping, spiraling up
to start all over

confident as a Cadillac, persistent
as one who knows she's got her work

cut out for her, who knows there are
not many willing to fly this high, be

this lonely.

The Necessity of Light

Flying through the black of a no-moon night
I suddenly fill with dread; perhaps I'm dying

perhaps I'm already dead and the wind
in my face, the chill in my bones

are tricks; that, in truth,
I no longer exist, ashes turned to black.
                      I try

for a sense of light and direction,
something to catch onto — wonder

if this is the long journey, the feared, quiet
trip we wait up all our lives for.
                                 When dawnlight,

finally, smears around sky's corner, faint
and careful then slow, strong

as an iron train swinging over the sky,
                how large I feel:

a meadow sweeping up to a foothill, a river
flowing like blood through my veins. At last

I see my good shadow flying blurred but definite
beneath me, skimming over a field so wild

there is no space for death, no room
for anything but roots and pulse of earth,

the blooming, and the light —
holding, releasing.

Wake Me. I'm Running Out of Dreams.

And now I stare into the open throat
of the sea, stare at the clean

snow covering mountains and think
what a beauty the world is

how everyone I've ever loved
has wanted it to stay that way:

unfouled, untampered with —
the dark releasing its flowers, its stars

the sea leaving its glittering and bony
parcels like gifts. And now I descend

>   over backs of mountains

>   over backs of oceans

>   over fog lifting its gray gauze from
fields of grain

>   over a speeding train

>   over a river pulling a boat slowly down
its spine

>   over a willow rinsing its green hair in
the river's basin

>   over a thin snake that slides down
a willow branch

        to stare into the black it will
slip to

slipping down
        to the everyday

slipping
        out of the spell, to another beginning.

Section II:

Black Car

Vision

I see all this: I see the pinch-faced
child hiding under the porch,
his father stamping around the yard
slapping a baseball bat onto his beefy

palm, screaming, "I'll kill that kid!"
the mother weeping against the porch
door screen and the younger sister
getting up from her nap, working

her toes into her Minnie Mouse slippers,
sliding open the glass door
of the gun cabinet in the den,
sliding open the middle desk drawer

where the bullets are and loading the gun
and padding over to the open window
in the dining room and aiming
and screaming, "I see you, Daddy,

I see you!..." again and again
until she believes she sees more than one
of him: one of him comes toward her, one
of him drops the bat, reels back,

one of him swims away into the long
raggedy grass of their front lawn
with an arm struck awkwardly in air as if he
were drowning, as if he were waving his hand

to ask permission, to find out from her
if it was all right, finally, to leave them alone.

Strangers—Late Summer Day

On a flickering summer lakeside lawn
a man unzips his windbreaker, running,
yelling as he runs and throwing his
belt like a snake, the man unwraps
like a gift as he runs to the thin cry

that had entered his head, as he enters
the water in his underwear and socks
splashing toward the woman with the open
red mouth, lungs forcing torn words
into air, her one hand raised

the man forgets his thwacking heart, forgets
that he is not a swimmer. As water rises,
rolls in the distance between his eyes
and the pink hand waving, the distance
closing, the man knows if he risked
not trying he would lose himself;

he swims to her, he touches her.

Looking in Windows

In the evening
when the lights come on
stories unfold
like a hand of cards:
the husband turning
his pockets out
as his wife's eyes tell
what's beyond reach.
The children's faces crumple
into sleep,
their bodies moving down
deep into their sleeping bags.
The TV's busted,
a pipe leaks
beneath the back porch,
waterfalls of ice
fanning out into the open garage.
          On the bedroom windows
fronds rise from the sills.
The man unbuckles his belt,
lies down beside her.
Nights like this
any warmth will do.
Under winter's dead weight
shadows grow long
across the bluish snow
as the moon rises
its glow like the light
of a television left on
all night in the other room.

Snow

The wife circles the table,
pours milk over Kix.

The father circles the house
in his beat-up Ford.

The kids hoot, slurp
as their spoons

circle the air like planes
passing over their childhoods.

The children have white moustaches.
Their father has a moustache.

Their mother has rings
under her eyes.

                She decides:
they cannot stay — last night

he phoned. Into
the snowsuits, out the door.

He circles the house.

She lifts the baby
into its carseat.

The children say nothing.
They sit still and quiet as ice.

It begins to snow.

Holding

Now that morning's here
everything grows — the lake
lifts its stars to the surface
as sunlight spreads.
Grass on the hill in back rises.
        She stands in his room
at the window. The sky is blue.
Something falls out of a cloud.
She folds clothes into boxes,
ties boxes with string. His toys
will not stay in their wooden chest;
they lift like black angels.
Sun crosses the room
as she touches wood.
                Outside
the lake presses hard like a fist
against the shore.

Violence

Clouds coming up fast now
trees expand their rings
leaves speed up —
lightning plugs in its
long extensions.
Fields of dry corn rasp
hard short breaths as
a man covers the open mouth
of a young girl. Sticks of
grass lay flat, twisted.
Black water
streams from the holes in the clouds.

Things

In Kanpur, India, a monsoon
drinks up children like soup.

In Mexico, the whole place goes at once,
lives sliding into slits forever shut.

And on a hot night in a Minnesota small town
a mother scoops peach ice cream

into bowls, the children, the father
waiting, laughing, telling knock-knocks.

It is 6:17 and out there
a tornado makes its decision: take

the house, leave them nothing.
                          The oldest girl, stopped

mid-joke, is first to hear the roar
of trains hitting the house —

teaspoons on the table jingling,
jumping

— the family dives into their concrete cellar.
Later, with a grace that surprises

both mother and father, they hold each other,
let go of things now lost

to wind, each one
taking in air, letting it go.

Television

Behind glass, the story spreads;
there is rumor of atrocities.
Our eye adjusts what it sees
to fit with the furniture.
In real life, the story is not
the same. There is blood on the road
to the Port-au-Prince airport
and we pretend a rainbow:
Haiti/bougainvillea/parrots
and those names:
Duvalier, Papa Doc, tontons macoute —
like drums, documents. Why
are we being told all this?
There is so much detail, we cannot
use it all. The TV glows steadily.
Behind glass, the story spreads,
grows. The eye adjusts.

In an Instant

                              It happens
as swiftly as the long-limbed way a dream

swims into your head and turns to flood,
a powerful forward push you cannot stem

or dilute with anti-dreams or anecdote:
Aunt Pauline's sure hunch her husband Luke

would outlive her because he was "too damn wild
to die" turned to dust

when he was killed, instantly, a sixty-year-old
barber-cum-cowboy whipping his black

stallion down the Interstate in the pitchdark
of four A.M., drunk as a coot. At the house

after the funeral, the other driver repeated
THERE WAS NO LIGHT, THERE WAS NO LIGHT once too

often, his pregnant young wife steering him out
of the kitchen.

Always, that possibility of surprise:
                      the way not one but

two geraniums came back to life after six
lightless months in the basement or the way

the fifty-five-year-old woman down the block,
having learned to ride her son's bike after

an entire summer of trying, trilled "I'm flying! I'm flying!"
as she swung past. How, just when I thought my life

capable only of unraveling, the telephone rang:
it was your voice soothing the hair back from my forehead

so I could breathe again, so
I could look out and see the moon brimming like silver

champagne over the black roads, the deep flashing river;
the huge barns in the distance solid, fast asleep over

their cows, hay, all the hidden things shining in the dark.

The Distant Flickering

*"Now my own life hits me in the throat, the bumps
And cuts of the walls as telling
As the poreholes in strawberries, tomato seeds..."*
  — Medbh McGuckian, "The Flitting"

She can't believe the things
that own her: mute, stable —
still, they conspire to lure
her halfway across a room

to fold linen into
perfect rectangles, roll
cotton socks into buns;
she likes the warm, round
weight of them in her hands,
that affinity with jugglers...

Now her life stares at her
from silver curves of spoons,
small cracks unzip along her
aging modest walls she disguises
with these knick-knacks, worn
brass, photographs of three
lanky teenage girls.

Standing before her window
she drinks the sky in as it moves
calmly over the dirt road
forgiving everything in its sway.
Carefully, she touches the welt
on her arm where his belt buckle
hit last week when she forgot to
lock the fierce hound, feathers
everywhere. One day, she thinks,

one day walking a dirt road
I will meet myself and I will
recognize immediately that part
of me that welcomes death—
holding my candle high, wax
spilling, dress reeking
wormwood and Lysol.
This is not more or less than
casual talk of making love
with someone you dislike
or getting even at all cost.
No less than if holding one's
breath resulted in living.
                        I'll wait—

long enough for my three to
spin their lives whole—wait
for them to step out fully-gowned
and higher-heeled to their roses.
Here in the fertile land I am
subsumed, settled as a thick
and well-earthed carrot,
immovable; my thin white root
probing down, down to where

vibrations of long-ago trains
are stored, rumbling empresses
plunging across the land
hungry for wilderness, wolves
sending up their howls like flares
above the distant flickering trees.

Black Car

Something long and dark glides
at the edge of my life

not something I see but feel
the way a blind girl

senses the heat of a wall to her left,
just out of reach of the *tap, tap*

of her stick. Even now, as we
drink cocktails — me in my bright

cotton dress, you in your crisp shirt
casually arranging boiled

shrimp on a blue plate — even now
I listen for a sleek swish, the hum

and click of the calm, expensive motor.
Finally, the doorbell rings, the party

careens to life. Cleverness abounds,
we laugh easily with each other,

a flush of movement: the lace of
conversation grows more intricate. A few

couples begin to dance, the neighbor we
just met jumps in the pool, everyone howls

— until at three A.M. the last
wobbly guest leaves me

to turn off the lights,
to enter the dark; to enter

my dreams that travel
the night. I recognize my fear

as it really is: a longing,
a dread as perplexing as this crazy-

quilt under whose soft folds I
each night lay my body

arranging my limbs so carefully
as if posed for sleep, holding

you so gently
as a carlight arcs wall to wall,

as the night begins its purring,
its soft ticking.

Section III:

Reconciliation Viewed from Great Distance

Greek Vases

                    Figures
lean from the vases: beneath

bands of shifting fretwork
a boy fishes for eel, two

girls weave cloth on a loom.
The women, bent over their trays

of fruit, receive advice
on home and silence. High

upon his tall-legged couch
an orator parts his lips

his profile shows one hollow
perfect eye, forefinger

forever in mid-air.
                On the next vase,

a woman holds a hand-mirror,
inspects her makeup:

the white lead she has smoothed
over her pale skin, the red

of alkanet root she has used
to blush her cheeks young again,

her mouth sealed with the fragrant
heaviness of wax. She remembers

the scarlet bird caught that morning
in her leather snare suddenly

freeing itself, red wings blinking
back the glare of morning sun

as it strained upward and soared
above the cold mountains

turning into air.

Going to Work

> *"I find it harder and harder every day
> to live up to my blue china."*
> — Oscar Wilde

Night into dawn.
Gray selves divide from houses,
slipping like mist
    to the larger streets

and you look up to see
lights, there and there,
opening a day.
        Other lives

tipped out of sleep:
feet on tile, ablutions,
creams—
        dream-husks

still attached, fragile as
this tea cup, determined as this
miniature Chinese girl who calls
    from under willows

to the boy poling his wooden
boat toward her —
the blue glaze of a century's
        daily touch

crackling, there and there,
at the rim.

After the Argument

My garden is littered
with tissue petals
of roses. Petunia bugles

have sucked themselves shut.
*You have decided to stay
with me.*

Peonies, soaked, lie
with pink jowls
pressed to earth —

each jagged blade cups
water. All day
we waited breathless

for this storm; it came
like a knife. Then,
an instant afterwards,

the air around us turned coolly
pure as lute music — water
strummed from the sky

sluicing off the roof
in sheets. As the world
turns on its back

to roll over, I turn
to brush aside the white sheet
to touch your breast

with my tongue; feel
you still here.

Shifting

How that windstorm two
summers ago transformed
her landscape: now, stark
windowless metal polesheds
replace forms of red wood
barns blown down,
autumn trees blaze their
belligerent color over twisted
trees the storm felled, chain-
saws hectoring each afternoon
of late fall. The sky swells,
plump with snow.
Cold air waits
at the edge of her heart
as afternoon light
changes to dusk and a black
night, seamless as cloth,
drops over the shifting landscape.
These are the hours
ghosts float up to tell her
how the land used to look,
the moments when she realizes
she must leave him, snow
beginning its inevitable slow
fall, blanket of whispers.

Insulation

This house is so closed up
we cannot hear the wintery wind.
Birds descend, peck

against the oak stump
but we can't hear them:
we are triple-glazed, secure.

I almost fail to notice you've
stalked out of the house,
again without coat or word

moist heat rising, collecting
in pulsing beads under attic
eave to burn and sting. I

travel familiar paths through
this house: pull fog from corners,
drag favorite props into view

force windows long-closed.
Suddenly
I want you to come back

to shelter you with my hair,
warm my skin with yours.
I wait for your boots

to stamp the back porch,
the room growing
as the iron latch lifts:

your eyes tell me
Careful. Go slow. The house
tightens its embrace.

Waiting for White

Look at the sky:
blowzy gray witches twirl
in tattered dresses
— between two steel posts
my cold sheets flap, last
leaves tilt and whirl in
gutters of my sleep.
Skies dim. Bells shiver.
The rapid breathing of
winter begins: dogs
of the town have picked it up
— pass it hound to hound.
Look at my house:
early evening turns it
the cobalt blue of milk-
of-magnesia bottles, its black
cellar smells of apples still
ripening in its corners as
I wait for snow, wait
for my windows to be calmed
by slipping hands of silver,
by thin curtains of white.
I feel I have waited like this
all my life.

Whitewash

Tonight everything is clear: loud crickets, air
still as a bowl of water, the light of the full
white moon generous in its clarity — all it touches
cleansed of sadness. Look how light sits
like white gold on my Chinese neighbor's melons
ripening behind his tool shed. On nights like this
it doesn't matter how shabby my house is
— the chiaroscuro makes all texture noble.
And I almost believe there is nothing hiding
under black leaves mounded on my lawn.
I imagine myself in my old bathrobe,
tightening the terrycloth belt, walking out my front
door into the rich night filling with kind animals
and strangers who raise arms to bless
as I pass silently by. The Chinese have a word
for the light that comes out of the eyes
when one is fully awake. Fully awake, I
need only stare at the gathering throngs
for them to know what is perfectly clear: that tonight,
at least, the world is safe.

Ceremony

He says *yes*
She says *yes*

—there is no turning back now,
organ climbing hill
after triumphant hill,
stained glass rages
into color. Guests smile
their exquisite formal
approval of love. Two
by two, they file out
behind the bride and groom

who for the first time
hear the loud wild bells
and know they can relax,
they can step out
of the photographer's frame

back into their plain bodies
which will branch
into each other

and each come
to understand the power
of words common as
yes, and again, *yes*

Reconciliation Viewed from Great Distance

Here is a town:
tiny houses
on streets thin
as mouse tails

A passenger train
jiggles away
into the blurred North

Someone on the edge
of the town
stands on her porch
waving a small shape
so white so important
the postman turns
comes back for it

The train continues
a line of ink
drawing toward the North

Near two A.M.
at the last station
a stick figure
small as a scratch
steps out
enters a cubicle
hesitates
dials

End of a Day,
End of a Summer

Long shadows of trees
beginning to recline

and the extravagant gesture of light
everywhere — on

teaspoons tinkling in saucers
on your face and hands

— the silver twinkle off the mast
of that one sailboat luffing

in the distance, the lake
throwing its rhinestones

and the pink roses nodding —
        a bird

gliding on a string of sun

water catching fire
as you take my hand.

Builders

One corner of her mouth a pouch
for nails, the other
tight and prim, she raises
her hammer again and again

pounding new nails into the new house,
sound pocking the air like buck-shot,
repeating itself in triplicate
against his kitchen window. Watching her

day after day methodically deplete
her stock of well-stacked bricks,
layered ships of wood, segmented
catacombs of nails, he wonders

as he dips plates, rinses
daily cups, shines glass
if his fork-and-knife acts
of maintenance are not also an art

if art can be indeed defined
as a skill of bringing order out of love
a belief
in the blueprints of dreams

and in the simplicity of things:
wall, window.
Cup, glass, spoon.

Night Fabrics

Tonight I stand on the same wooden porch
my aunts Marvel and Beryl used
for their spying and listening
after twinned hours of quilting, crocheting —

and I become a sounding board for zizzing crickets,
the slow-rising of toads.
A drift of fireflies floats a swag
of organdy pulled by invisible wires,
pinpoints of white light spreading
across marsh, the tall-grassed fields,
flowing in slow determination over the dark

where there is no measurable logic —
only lace of night wind
swathing the thick-knitted
plots of night.

Grandmother Poaching
Pears with Cloves

It is 6:30 P.M.

Already, her diabetic son Lars
grumbles about tomorrow's weather,
today's luck; Jack Benny
yammering on the radio "Now Rochester
(pause pause pause) CUT that out!"
and Jesus praying so simply above
the egg-head photograph of Eisenhower,
both bathed in the pole-lamp's
megaphoned light. It was a house of
knick-knacks and things being saved,
scoured, re-done. Grandmother measured
my height, taught crochet, make-do
told me my future was a problem
to be solved later, in high school,
with typing and shorthand

and shocked me to my bones that day
when something seemed to break inside her
and she screamed how she hated cooking—
    had always hated cooking—
  wished she'd never set eyes
on a fry-pan, slamming one down on her
enamel-top table.

Grandmother, leaning her square back
against the door of her new Frigidaire,
breathed heavily and—for the moment
herself again

—handed Lars and me the bowls,
spoons, a pitcher of cream.
Carefully, we set them on the table,
silently swallowed the warm spiced pears.

Polio: 1953

I didn't want that young girl to die
in her long cylinder of steel

because, for one thing, she loved
the way the light fell over Serpent Lake,

the way her parent's green lawn
slid down to water's edge almost as though —

if it hadn't been caught — it would have
kept going. The girl loved to run, the pull

of wind on her hair. Now,
as her face dozes in the mirror clamped

above her, she listens to the machine
as it breathes for her during this long night

where she races over endless, unfamiliar hills
and knows she will not slow

until she sees water soundless and
glittering before her; knows

she can get ready to slide, to stop running,
start the fierce, awkward thrashing

arm-over-arm through black, over black. On a
distant hill, the roof of her house expands

and contracts over her mother and father, asleep;
her dog, asleep; the door to her empty room

carefully opening.

The Parents Are Leaving

They think we don't need them anymore
so they are quietly departing this world
through black slits in night skies
or as dust motes, rising to the sun.
They do, however, return.
My mother still climbs a stairway
to check if I sleep
or if I want. My mother, dead
eight months now, her eyes, her hands
still searching for peace, she
dances swift then slow in the air
of this high-winded autumn morning.
We are part of the same waltz, time
suspends us in its midst: autumn
trails summer, winter
behind autumn, I follow roads
my ancestors followed,
scattering their bounty. Outdoors,
my mother bends with the trees
setting down without ceremony
small crackling gifts.

Veterans Hospital — 1989

The hospital moves
like a ship through the night
its colossal motor churns

passengers enter half-sleep
as fog rises past windows
                        Breath

a preoccupation — the bodies
filling with air
            the narrow escape:

my father's pre-breakfast quip
"one more day in the swamp"
his shy grin of relief
                      Tonight

as my father sleeps
his restless hands clench
and unclench the rope of wet sheet

his eyes wide open
as if he sees past me
into the distance

eyes intent, unblinking, as if
watching a film
impossible not to watch

the scene where the alarm sounds
the heavy furniture unhooking
slithering across the floor

every man for himself

Visiting the Graves—February

Everyone here sleeps:
as spring sleeps still
in hard centers
of these midwestern hills,
as sawdust hearts sleep
in beeches. No last leaves
trickle down.

Beneath the ground,
bones of those who came
before me.

Their voices return:
those I knew throb
in my own voice,

those I did not
still circle the earth
spilling their song. Snow

begins,
falling heavily. Sky
generous as my Norwegian
grandmothers, Anna and Anna,
their bowls of thick white
cream for pale coffee.

The day darkens.
All around
lights in the houses
come on one by one.

       I walk through
shadow cross-hatching
this cemetery, away
from bones of those
for whom I hold such
tenderness in my heart

for having been there first
for having left first
for having left me
  here
under these brief, unfinished stars.

Section IV:

Words

It Hid Motionless Like

a scream among black leaves and waited.
Its event didn't take long, dogs
grinning, straining against their blood-
lines and so we sat for six hours
under the station lights proving that
innocence doesn't exist. I watched
it all and now I am watching it again,
the darkness large and surprisingly
strong. I sit with a butcher knife
in my lap.

You Cannot Believe

this; I had to bribe it to get it
to come to me — so exhausted, sullen,
too weary to move. We poked its
underparts with a stick. It was not
exactly pretty but, you know, its
rhythm was intoxicating; we could not
get it to stop wriggling, its breath
silver as light, so different from
the accidents flying over us
each morning when we don't look.
I knelt to touch its slit, happy
to discover I could believe.

Twiddle with Its

dials; it has a sophisticated
appreciation of your rapt attention.
Whatever you do, do not let go
of the dilator or you will find
the entire mechanism will turn
on you, reinvent your past. I
warn you, beware the subjunctive.
You'll find it dangling from its
underparts like some unnecessary
appendage but, believe me, it is not:
press the two peach-colored bars,
it will become part of your history.

One Green One Red Lens: Serial in Five Parts

If there was a movie unreeling, it could be now. It's only that the cogs keep on jamming; there is a weird stutter. It makes for pixilation on the screen which only adds to the overall picture. Pluto the dog has a tongue wrapped around Porky Pig's dainty trotters. When Porky trips he lands "S-S-S-Say!" on his pink butt. The entire horizon is turning and turning peach or not peach. If we walk toward, it recedes to technicolor.

My father's hairline goes up until he wears a hat; he stares hard at what is before him. In his hat he can carry quite a bit, all he owes. There is only so much we can take. The heat can be overturning. Adjectives, barriers to the overall plot. Here, a floorplan; a long couch some call a settee or davenport stands on its tippy-toes. As I walk, it staggers away into its far north. What special effects. We went and stood outside.

The tornado didn't hit us; it passed up. Just grew. There goes that yellow house with the blue door. Yo-yos, frisbees, those little red houses for monopoly. Trouble was, he always wanted to take back the conversation. Wasn't easy converting francs to yen then again to money. I could be red wrong but it's true he has trouble handling finances. So what if the slides were not ours, were someone else's holiday. Everyone today has a camera. Pictures almost real as postcards. Some years, one didn't need to go.

> We raised money to send twin boys to cystic fibrosis camp. It's "too real." It "really meant a lot to them two." We keep track of associations one to another. A postcard of a train hitting a house like a tornado looks like natural

disaster. House with rooms, windows, a blue door. Two small boys gasping for breath. I used the long couch as excuse for a train when nothing else. History, distance, a where to go to. Calling for the very best in us.

> Our best hats. Gloves. Tickets. Hands to our eyes and the cardboard glasses, one green one red lens. Everything zonged to dimension. Something real to this. Vincent Price pawing the wax window, blood running over the sill. Hiss, plausibility,

applause. Coming from black to light blue, big white clouds, planes on vacation lounge the far range in the north. And the real weather within us, ticking within. The for-instances we take for granted. If we don't talk about them they won't be. No black or white. Colorization of films takes Humphrey Bogart's breath away, as if on holiday. He still smokes, wears a hat.

Words

*"words are strong, too,
stronger than rocks or steel
stronger than potatoes, corn, fish, cattle,
and soft, too, soft as little pigeon-eggs."*
— Carl Sandburg

Out beyond my road a word
Stretches toward the farthest mountain.
I walk small. There is no word here
For town, street.

Only silo, corn. Words born alone
Die alone. There are the crops to think of,
The rise and fall of, ripening,
Spilling out of their husks, splitting

Their green sleeves, scratching their
White wrists for the sound.

*

I've forgotten how words expand in heat,
The uneasy fit of words with other words.
One word, exhausted miles before arriving,
Collapsed and died. That was just example.
Most words do what they were hired to:

One word dips its fingers in blood and
Smears its walls.
Another is wary of our phobias:
When that word opens, it is a choir
Spilling into the street
Urging us to stay out of the sun, drink plenty
Of water, lie down in a cool dry place, remember
That when words run too hard, too exquisitely
Hard, they disappear forever.

*

postcard:

"My number came up quick. I boarded with my words intact, stamped. Thank God. I should be in Trieste in 4 days. Wait for me. I bring word."

x

✽

Alone as I am in the brown study
(words face-down on the windowsill)

A fine young word rides by on horseback

(with a whip) Now the door shuts and it's
time to start: dressed (in a dress)

shoed (with shoes) my life depends
on the...............of words

under the gray linen (fog) low
weighted syllables dangle to

watch a word through glass
ride steadily over (what could be) water

or fire or snow or (more) words

※

The girl holding her gifts close,
she ran with squirrels, buffalo, antelope,
moles, ran with her words, pressing on
to where ships burned, armies
marched over graves of other armies;
past bears, their paws plunging for fish;
past storks rising, past tortoises
struggling out of their shells as

a pebble drops down a well, a tree tilts,
a sentence ends. At last a drowsiness and
dream ending, a road turning in innuendo
and inflection, the girl holding her words
to tide-flow, ocean wash; she has come
from great distance to cold gong of ship bell,
the girl bearing her gift, these words.

*

in kitchen roast word burns as host
kisses caterer unhooking thin words
of bra his words on breasts down one
long hall a word rolls there are
games in Rec Room Darcy waltzes with
platter words and hard rolls curved
jug of stout her hard curved breasts
words anyone? her laughter tinkles
tickles tackles ANY ONE WORD? her
heart knocks last Ed takes one Fred
takes Snood takes there is fire look-
ing for fireplace to start flames
question what word on tip? yes or no
Audrey beams blooms Lloyd blushes sh-
ushes rolling r's into dark stout arms
he would waltz Audrey or Darcy rock'n
roll flames on tapedeck ANYONE? he
blurts blats booms two and three hot
games of craps corners room cigarette
burns on carpet Lorraine draws Lem to
cold tile floor of bathroom licking
his word loosening tie long drawn out
word rolls down hall guests drink words
abandon tear chunks hard rolls crumbs
scatter carpet burns whole slowly going
up in

※

They tell me a dead word
Sinks so slowly its body
Decomposes
Before it touches bottom

Silvery, dreamy, it could
Be anything: the word unconscious
Becomes the sea's quiet
Breathing. Or the word

Rises abruptly, its jaws open,
Blackmailing us against the rocks
For days, fine pebbles falling
Beneath our toe-holds, hand-holds,
Its hot breath
Brands itself into our heads

※

Rugged tongued, so
Huge in height and width

Our words extend out to the hills.
Some have candles. Some, bells.

The wind, impartial, writes its long
Letter long into the night

Where it is always safe,
Where it is black with tongues

Checking our errors, adjusting,
Erasing.

Patricia Zontelli grew up on the Cuyuna Range in northern Minnesota. She graduated from the University of Minnesota with an M.F.A in Studio Art. Ten years ago, living in London, she signed up for a poetry workshop at Goldsmiths College and was immediately seduced by the reading, the writing of poetry. A former Loft Mentor Series winner, she lives in Menomonie, Wisconsin and teaches at the University of Wisconsin-Stout.

About her writing, Patricia Zontelli says: "This is the task: to write poems that have music and magic; to write poetry that matters. I write to discover, an attempt to find the link between the visible and invisible, reality and dream. Poetry has become a passion. The best advice I ever got about writing: do it every day."

3198A

NORMANDALE COMMUNITY COLLEGE
LIBRARY
9700 FRANCE AVENUE SOUTH
BLOOMINGTON, MN 55431-4399